Anonymous

Observations on Mr. Burke's Speech on Mr. Fox's India Bill

In an address to that Gentleman

Anonymous

Observations on Mr. Burke's Speech on Mr. Fox's India Bill
In an address to that Gentleman

ISBN/EAN: 9783337059217

Printed in Europe, USA, Canada, Australia, Japan

Cover: Foto ©ninafisch / pixelio.de

More available books at **www.hansebooks.com**

OBSERVATIONS

ON

MR. BURKE's SPEECH

ON

MR. FOX's

INDIA BILL,

IN AN ADDRESS

TO THAT

GENTLEMAN.

AUDI ALTERAM PARTEM.

LONDON:
PRINTED FOR THE AUTHOR, M,DCC,LXXXIV.

OBSERVATIONS

ON

Mr. BURKE's SPEECH, &c.

SIR,

THERE was a time when your plausibility imposed on the world, and when the public mistook your specious professions for real integrity. The delusion is now past; and if your conduct had not taught me to distrust all your actions, and to disbelieve all your assertions, I might have been foolish enough to have given you some credit for your zeal in promoting Mr. Fox's India Bill, and for your candour in publishing your speech. I might have been weak enough to think, that, touched by the sufferings of the oppressed natives of India, your sensibility had warmed you to a vehemence of language, which your cooler moments had condemned; and that reflecting on the mean-

 ness

neſs of detracting characters, in a place where you could not be called to an account, you had generouſly determined to publiſh your ſpeech, in order to afford an opportunity of anſwering your abuſe, and obviating your calumny. I ſay, Sir, ſuch might have been my opinion of your motives on the preſent occaſion, if you had not made it manifeſt to me and all the world, that talking is your *trade*; that you have long ago bartered every principle of honour, for the ſordid conſideration of ſelf intereſt; that the invectives of your ſpeech were dictated as much by the malevolence of your diſpoſition, as in aid of your party; and that your vanity and malignity excited you to publiſh it. By the former you were flattered with a belief, that your oratory would dignify abuſe; and by the latter you were led to hope, that though your falſehoods might not paſs without detection, yet they would make an impreſſion to the prejudice of the Company and their ſervants.

I MIGHT almoſt truſt to the univerſal contempt of your character, for an aſſurance that your ſpeech will be little read, and leſs regarded: But ſince it has become a general practice, to impute to the Eaſt India Company and their ſervants, every ſpecies of crime that can diſgrace the human character, and ſince you, Sir, have been particularly guilty of this unjuſtifiable liberty, I ſhall take leave to offer a few ſhort remarks on ſome palpable

pable falſehoods, which you have ventured to give to the public as abſolute facts: I ſhall paſs over the greateſt part of your affected declamation (for it cannot be called reaſoning) on the *chartered rights of men*, and content myſelf with obſerving on ſuch parts only, as have ſomething like argument for their ſupport. In page 9 you ſay, "I ground my-"ſelf on this principle, that if the abuſe is proved, "the contract is broken, and we re-enter into all "our rights." An Engliſh lawyer will tell you, Sir, that your principle is erroneous, and that a charter does not become forfeited, though its privileges ſhould be abuſed. But I will not avail myſelf even of your errors: I will combat your poſition in its moſt extenſive meaning, and anſwer it by ſaying, you muſt, in juſtice and in equity, *prove* the abuſe, before you can act on your own principles. Now, Sir, I repeat what you heard at the bar of the Houſe, in the Houſe, and out of it, a thouſand times, that the abuſe has *not been proved*, that it has never been *attempted to be proved*, and that it is *not even ſtated* in the preamble of the bill, which deſtroy's the Company's charter. In the ſame page you add, "When we have perfected the plan laid "down before us by the right honourable mover, "the world will then ſee *what it is we deſtroy, and* "*what it is we create.*" Thank God, the world ſaw *before* you had *perfected* your *plan*, what you meant to deſtroy, and what you meant to create; and by this foreſight, you have been prevented

 from

from destroying the rights of the Company, and creating an unconstitutional power in the English government. I am not very ambitious of coinciding with you in opinion, for very obvious reasons, and therefore when I do agree with you in any sentiment, I shall not be suspected of partiality. As a proof of it, I entirely accede to your observation, that "nothing is to be found in any habits "of life or education, which tends wholly to disqualify men for the functions of government, "but a spirit and habit of low cabal and intrigue, "which are never united with a capacity for sound "and manly policy." This is so very just, that I perfectly agree with you, no instance of it was ever seen; and I do verily believe, that if your vanity would permit you to see yourself, you would not make an exception to this general rule even in your own favour.

In page 12, you assert, that "With *very few*, "and those *inconsiderable*, intervals, the British "dominions, either in the Company's name, or "in the names of Princes absolutely dependent "upon the Company, extend from the mountains "that separate India from Tartary, to Cape Comorin, that is one and twenty degrees of latitude." Now, Sir, in Major Rennel's excellent map, from whence I doubt not you derived all this geographical knowledge, which you so wonderfully displayed for the edification of the country gentlemen, I observe,

serve, not the *inconsiderable intervals*, but the extensive kingdoms of the Mahrattas, the Rajah of Berar, the Soubah of the Deccan, Hyder Ally, Nudiff Khan, the Seiks, the Jauts, and Abdallah Khan, which are totally independent of the Company, and which comprise full two thirds of that vast tract, that you give to the Company—Not that they may abuse the gift, but that you may abuse them. This remark I make, not for the sake of cavilling at such trifles, as 14 or 15 degrees of latitude, but merely to shew, that when you wish to deal in round numbers and round assertions, you make no scruple of sinking kingdoms in your account, or destroying them by famine in your description. In your own words, "so far with "regard to the extent;" now to the population, which, as you observe, "is not easy to be calcu-"lated:" but availing yourself of that facility of calculation and assertion, which you so easily make to suit your purpose, you add, in page 13, "When "the countries of which it is composed, came into "our possession, they were *all* eminently well "peopled, and eminently productive, though at "that time considerably declined from their antient "prosperity. But since they are come into our "hands!——!" Here, Sir, you were stopped, no doubt, by your humanity; and your amiable sensibility shews itself in the beautiful ellipsis you have chosen to interrupt and adorn your fiction. But as I am a plain unlettered man, not versed in the

powers

powers or figures of rhetoric, let me acquaint you with a simple historical account of *those countries* which did come in our possession. I must observe, that in this page, you have been *studiously* and artfully obscure. If your calculation of thirty millions, include *all* the countries from Tartary to Cape Comorin, you must subtract twenty millions for the countries I have proved not to belong to us, and I must again reduce your *round* numbers to the kingdom of Bengal, Bahar, and a very small part of Orissa. Now, Sir, attend to the account which an *historian on the spot, gives of these provinces, so eminently productive, and so eminently peopled.

"These laws continued in full force till the in-
"vasion of Nadir Shah, and till that time, there
"was scarce a better administered government in
"the world. The manufactures, commerce, ag-
"riculture, flourished exceedingly; and none felt
"the hand of oppression, but those who were dan-
"gerous by their wealth or power: But when
"the governors of the provinces found the weak-
"ness of the Mogul, and each set up as sovereign
"in his own province, although they could not
"break through these immutable laws, *they inven-*
"*ted new taxes under new names*; which doubled
"or trebled the original ones, and which the

* Scrafton's Indostan, page 25, printed 1763.

"landholder

" landholder was obliged to levy on his tenants. " The old ſtock of wealth for ſome time ſupported " this; but when that failed, and the tenants were " ſtill preſſed for more, they borrowed of uſurers, " at an exorbitant intereſt; and the government " ſtill continuing theſe demands, the lords of the " lands were obliged to do the ſame: but as all " this while the value of the lands did not increaſe, " the conſequence was, that at laſt, unable to pay " the intereſt of the mortgages, the *rents were* " *ſeized by rapacious uſurers.* The government " finding the revenues fall ſhorter every year, at " laſt *ſent collectors and farmers of the revenues into* " *the provinces.* Thus the lord of the land was " diveſted of the power over his country, and the " tenants expoſed to *merciless plunderers*; till the " farmer and manufacturer finding the more they " laboured the more they paid, the manufacturer " would work no more, nor the farmer cultivate " no more than was neceſſary for the *bare ſubſiſtence* " of his family. *Thus this once flouriſhing and plen-* " *tiful country, has, in the courſe of a few years,* " *been reduced to ſuch miſery, that many thouſands* " *are continually periſhing through want.* The " crown lands are ſtill worſe off, let out to the " higheſt bidder; and the jaghire lands alone re- " main unplundered. Hence that equal diſtribu- " tion of wealth that makes the happineſs of a peo- " ple, and ſpreads a face of cheerfulneſs and plen- " ty through all ranks, *has now ceaſed*; and the

" riches

" riches of the country are ſettled partly in the " hands of a few uſurers and greedy courtiers, and " the reſt *is carried out of the country* by the foreign " troops, taken into pay *to maintain the governors* " *in their uſurpation.* This unhappy decay the " India Company have already experienced, in the " decline of their trade, and the riſe and price of " their manufactures, and will, I fear, *experience* " *more and more annually.*"

Another *hiſtorian ſays, " The country was " torn to pieces by civil wars, and groaned under " every ſpecies of domeſtic confuſion. Villainy " was practiſed in every form ; all law and religion " were trodden under foot ; the bands of private " friendſhips and connections, as well as of ſociety " and government, were broken ; and every indi- " vidual, as if amidſt a foreſt of wild beaſts, could " rely upon nothing but the ſtrength of his own " arm."

This, Sir, is the account of theſe flouriſhing and proſperous countries, *before the Company had any ſhare in their management.* But as you may not, perhaps, approve of authorities that ſo flatly contradict your deſcription, allow me to appeal to another, to whom you can have no objection : I mean, Sir, the unqueſtionable Mr. Philip

* Dow's Hiſtory of Hindoſtan, Appendix, page 57.

Francis ;

Francis; the man, according to your own deſcription, "whoſe deep reach of thought, whoſe "large legiſlative conceptions, and whoſe grand "plans of policy, make the moſt ſhining parts of "your reports." After informing you that every department of the ſtate had gone into confuſion, from the death of Sujah Khan, in the year 1739; after telling you of the depredations of the uſurper Ally Verdy Khan, of the ravages and incurſions of the Mahrattas, of the invaſion of the Shah Zadah, (the preſent Emperor,) the rebellion of the Nabob of Purneah, and many other Zemindars, or in your phraſe, native Princes, of the war with Coſſim Ally Khan, and the irruption of Sujah Dowlah into Bahar, he ſays, in his minute of the 22d of July, 1776, "It muſt be evident from the preceding "ſtate of facts, when the dewannee was ceded to "the Company, the country was already in a very "reduced condition, by a quick ſucceſſion of wars "and revolutions, large ſums carried away, *ancient "eſtabliſhments overthrown, great numbers of Zemin-"dars diſpoſſeſſed and reduced to beggary, and heads "of families murdered.* It would be an endleſs and diſguſting fatigue, to follow you minutely thro' all your labyrinths of miſrepreſentation, and therefore I ſhall diſmiſs your next paragraph as to the quality and deſcription of the inhabitants, with remarking, that it is a pretty fanciful paſſage, which will do very well to adorn your next edition of the ſtory of little Red Riding Hood.

In page 16, you boldly aſſert, "I engage myſelf to you, to make good theſe poſitions. Firſt, "I ſay, that from Mount Imaus to Cape Comorin, "there is not a *ſingle* Prince, ſtate or potentate, "great or ſmall, with whom they have come in "contact, whom they have not ſold. Secondly, "I ſay, there is not a *ſingle* treaty they have ever "made, which they have not broken. Thirdly, "I ſay, that there is not a ſingle Prince or ſtate, "who ever put their truſt in the Company, who "is not utterly ruined:" and theſe aſſertions, you add, are in the "full ſenſe *univerſal*." Now, Sir, if I had not a much greater regard to decency, than you have ſhewn on this and many other occaſions, I ſhould not content myſelf with barely ſaying that every aſſertion is falſe; I ſhould uſe a much harſher epithet: but the dignity of my own character, forbids me imitating ſo unworthy an example. The pledges you have offered to the Houſe, have been ſo notoriouſly made to anſwer the purpoſe of the day, that they are no more regarded, than the cries of the ſhepherd in the fable. Witneſs your repeatedly engaging yourſelf to bring Lord North to the block: Witneſs your engaging yourſelf to prove Mr. Haſtings a delinquent. Have you yet done either? And will you ſtill dare to inſult the Houſe and the public, with theſe empty boaſts? But that you may not have the ſhadow of a plea for the preſumption of this ſolemn engagement, I will prove that the reverſe

of

of your propoſition is the truth. Major Scott, in his reply to your ſpeech, has proved the falſehood of your aſſertion, and your panegyric on "the "*great*" Mogul; and therefore I have only to add, that this "high perſonage" had been a ſtate priſoner, together with his father and all the family, in the hands of the Vizier of Oude; that he had been deprived of his throne, his kingdom, and his crown, for years before the Company had the management of the country; that he had been perſecuted by the Vizier, till, as he ſaid in a letter to Colonel Clive, "*he had not left him a ſpot "to reſt on;" that in diſtreſs and indigence, he applied to Lord Clive in the year 1765, who aſſigned him the provinces of Corah and Allahabad, with a ſtipend of twenty-ſix lacks of rupees. Theſe he enjoyed as long as he remained under our protection, which was the *condition* of the aſſignment: And I would wiſh you to remark, Sir, that this high perſonage, on *quitting our protection*, fell again into that miſery from which we had reſcued him, and is, unfortunately for you and himſelf, a ſtriking inſtance to prove the falſeneſs of your aſſertion: for *he broke the treaty* with the Company: *he truſted the Company*, and was affluent whilſt he confided in that truſt; *he withdrew it himſelf*, transferred it to the Mahrattas, and *then*, and *only then*, was ruined.

*Scrafton's Indoſtan, pages 112 and 118.

MAJOR

Major Scott has repeatedly refuted your assertion of the sale of the Rohillas, and therefore I shall pass it over, to come to your *account sales* in page 19; and here, Sir, it is impossible (to use your own elegant apostrophe) not to pause for a moment, to reflect on the falsity and futility of this paragraph, where there is such a trifling childish play on the word *sale*, that one would really imagine it had made the same impression on your sensorium, as the word *whiskers* did on the Queen of Navarre in Tristram Shandy, and that you had indulged yourself in a parody of that ludicrous author, rather than been speaking on an important subject to an august assembly. Really, Sir, it is difficult to consider with temper, either the matter of this paragraph, or the manner in which you have expressed it. The tyrant Surajah Dowlah, who perhaps may have recommended himself to you, by his inhuman murder of an hundred of the *Company's servants*, not only never fulfilled the conditions of his treaty with the Company, but had scarcely concluded it, †when he wrote for Monsieur Bussy, who commanded a large French army in the Deccan, with whom he intended to join his forces, and attack us the moment Admiral Watson's squadron and forces left the river. He kept a large army at Plassy: He ordered Meer Jaffier to join it with a large body of troops, and

†Scrafton's Indostan, pages 70 and 83.

promised

promiſed him ten lacks of rupees, if he proved victorious. He ſent for Monſieur Laws from Patna, to aſſiſt him in this enterprize. He turned our ambaſſador out of his court. He protected openly the French troops under Monſieur Laws, whilſt we were at war with that nation, and allowed that gentleman ten thouſand rupees a month. He ſearched the factory at Coſſimbuzar, in time of profound peace. He refuſed a free paſſage to the Engliſh through the country, and would not pay more than a fifth part of the ſum, which, by treaty, he bound himſelf to diſcharge, for his ſhameful and unjuſtifiable plunder of Calcutta. Theſe, Sir, were the real cauſes of renewing the war with Surajah Dowlah, which you are not aſhamed to call a breach of treaty of the Engliſh Company, and a ſale of that inhuman tyrant. Meer Jaffier had married a ſiſter of Ally Verdy Khan, and from this alliance he was pointed out, both by the miniſters and the principal officers of the army, as the propereſt perſon to ſucceed to the muſnud, on which he was placed after the battle of Plaſſy. He had not been ſeated there long, when, the *hiſtorian I have already quoted, ſays, " He ſeemed to look on us rather as rivals " than allies; and his firſt thoughts were how to " check our power, and *evade the execution of the* " *treaty.*" After enumerating many inſtances of

*Scrafton's Indoſtan, page 99.

perfidy

perfidy in Meer Jaffier, and exhibiting what he justly calls "*a scene of plots and conspiracies, "wherein the several actors displayed the arts of "treachery and dissimulation, with all the refined "subtility of eastern politicians," he relates the invasion of the Shah Zadah, (present Mogul,) who had been joined by the forces of the Soubah of Oude's brother, and the French party under Monsieur Laws. With this army he laid siege to the city of Patna, and was very near carrying the place, when the appearance of Colonel Clive obliged him to raise it. "†Thus," continues Mr. Scrafton, "was the Soubah once more indebted "to us for his life and government, both which "must have inevitably fallen, but for this vigorous effort; for so little able was he to *support* "*himself*, that far from joining, his troops surrounded him, and refused to march, till they "had all their arrears, and two months pay advanced them." This weak Prince, who, so far from being *ruined* by the *trust* he put in the Company, according to your doctrine, was, from the beginning of his reign, unable to exist without their protection; and in a few years, had brought both the Company and the country into such a distressful situation, by his misconduct and mismanagement, that certain destruction would have attended both, if he had not been removed from

*Scrafton's Indostan, page 105. †Ibid, page 115.

his adminiſtration. For at this time Mr. Vanſittart, who was the author of the revolution in favour of Meer Coſſim, declares, that " *his affairs " were in ſo confuſed and impoveriſhed a ſtate, " that in all human appearance, another month " could hardly have run through, before he would " have been cut off by his own Seapoys, and the " city become a ſcene of plunder and diſorder, the " Nabob having made no further proviſion for " the payment of the long arrears due to his peo- " ple, after Coſſim Ally Khan had freed him " from his former extremity;" when his life was threatened, and would have been taken away, by his mutinous troops, if Coſſim had not, at " †that " time, paid a large ſum out of his own treaſury." Jaffier not only *evaded* the treaty he made with the Company, as Mr. Scrafton relates, but he *violated it* in ſeveral inſtances. ‡He had been ſcarce ſeated in his government, when he entered into a ſecret negociation with the Dutch, to introduce an armament in the provinces, to deſtroy our power and influence. He meditated a ſecret treaty with the Shah Zadah, and offered to ſacrifice us to that Prince. §He alſo was near carrying into execution a ſecret treaty with the Mahrattas, which would have proved the total deſtruction of the country, if it had not been prevented. ‖ Notwithſtanding

*Holwell's Tracts, 3d edition, page 95. †Ibid. ‡Ibid, p. 21.

§Ibid. ‖ Ibid, p. 95 and 96.

theſe

these instances of infidelity and ingratitude, the government of Bengal were averse from taking violent measures against Meer Jaffier: but at last his conduct became so weak and wicked, that Mr. Vansittart and his committee, had no other alternative, than either to lose the country, or remove him from his government. In this critical situation, they resolved to transfer the administration to his son in law, Cossim Ally Khan; and Meer Jaffier came down to Calcutta, where he was received and treated with all possible respect and attention; and where, as the *Governor observes in his letter to the council, "the days of his ease "did him more honour, than those of his power." In this situation he remained quiet and happy, till the war with Cossim Ally Khan broke out, when he was again restored to the musnud, and soon after died. To him succeeded his son Nudjum ul Dowlah, who lived but a short time, and was succeeded by his brother Syf ul Dowlah, who likewise died very soon; and to him succeeded his younger brother, the present Nabob, Mobaruk ul Dowlah. Not a tittle of the treaties with any of these Princes has been broken; and though they may not have lived in as much splendor as their predecessors, it is certain they have lived in sufficient affluence, and with much more ease and happiness.

*Original Papers printed for Newbury 1765, Letter 4.

In this very particular account of bargain and ſale, which you have given to prove your ſecond and third *univerſal* aſſertions, of a *ſingle treaty* never having been made, which had not been broken, nor a ſingle Prince or ſtate, who ever put any truſt in the Company, not being ruined, it is ſomewhat ſingular that you ſhould omit Sujah Dowlah, the Soubah of Oude; his rank in the empire, certainly entitled him to the next place to that "high perſonage," the Great Mogul: but perhaps you were ſo dazzled by looking at this pinnacle of "*human veneration*," that you were blind to an inferior object. Allow me, therefore, to preſent him to your recovered ſenſes, as another inconteſtible proof of the falſity of your aſſertions. The Company not only never violated the treaty with him, but, as General Smith and Sir Robert Barker will tell you, who commanded the army on two different occaſions, preſerved his dominions from the invaſions of the Mahrattas. Nay, more, Sir; by his alliance with the Company, he gained more territory, and died in poſſeſſion of more wealth than any of his predeceſſors.

Major Scott has refuted and expoſed all the reſt of your jargon of ſales of the Mahrattas and Ragobah, the Paiſhwa and Rajah of Berar, &c. He has alſo replied to the moſt material parts of the reſt of your ſpeech; and as you have been ſufficiently convicted of miſrepreſentation, to diſcredit the whole of your performance, I ſhould take my leave of you, ſatisfied with the aſſurance, that thoſe who will be at the trouble of reading this Letter, will be convinced I have made good my promiſe, of proving from hiſtorical facts, the falſity of your aſſertions; but, Sir, impoſſible as it is, to follow your wild imagination with any degree of regularity, or to ſoar as high as your fertile genius carries you into the regions of fancy and fiction, I cannot forbear an attempt to attend your flight a little farther, though at an humble diſtance.

In the notice you take of the Company's internal government, you draw a compariſon between it, and that of the conquerors who preceded us in India; and after indulging yourſelf, as uſual, in many rhetorical flouriſhes and ſimilies, amongſt which you can find none ſo ſuitable to the Company and their ſervants, as the ourang, outan, and the tiger, you kindly decide in favour of the Arabs, Tartars, and Perſians. You then draw a hideous caricature of the gentlemen who go to India, and having loaded them with every term of abuſe, both in metaphor and hyperbole, you apologize, with your native modeſty, to truth and nature, for the moderation of your temper; and with the ſame unaſſuming grace aſſure us, that you are thus gentle, for fear of being thought like Tacitus and Machiavel, not to diſapprove of the crimes you deſcribe. Here are no leſs than three

pages

pages of intolerable abuſe, on the *boys*, as you call them, who are ſent to India; but happily for them, not a word of truth in the whole; and I cannot conceive why you ſhould have been ſo very ſplenetic with the poor lads, unleſs ſome of them, or their maſters, may have offended you, and, like Drawcanſir, you are determined,

Should any of the Gods be ſo uncivil,
You'll make that God ſubſcribe himſelf a Devil.

The next thirty pages are a ſummary of the rancour of your curious fabrication called reports, to which Major Scott and Detector, have both ably and amply replied. I ſhall, therefore, very willingly paſs over them, to come to a part of your ſpeech, which has ſome little appearance of reaſoning in it; and that is where you ſtate the conduct of the Company towards the landed intereſt. In page 67, you ſay, "So early as 1769, "the Company's ſervants perceived the decay into "which thoſe provinces had fallen under *Engliſh* "*adminiſtration*, and they made a ſtrong repreſen-"tation upon this decay, and what they appre-"hended to be the cauſe of it. Soon after Mr. "Haſtings became Preſident of Bengal, the landed "intereſt of a whole kingdom was ſet up to public "auction. Mr. Haſtings ſet up the whole nobi-"bility, gentry, and freeholders, to the higheſt "bidders. No preference was given to the an-

"cient

" cient proprietors." I am ſorry, Sir, to be ſo frequently obliged to uſe ſuch expreſſions as your aſſertions force from me; but in the cauſe of truth and innocence, I cannot forbear to ſpeak plainly, and muſt tell you, Sir, that the firſt part of this paragraph is a miſrepreſentation, and the laſt not the fact.

IN the year 1765, the grant of the dewannee was made to the Company, and the management of the provinces was committed to three *native miniſters*, jointly with Mr. Sykes, the Reſident at the Durbar. Mahommed Reza Khan was, however, both the *oſtenſible* and *efficient* miniſter. The ſyſtem which he adopted for collecting the revenues, was a very pernicious one of Coſſim Ally Khan's; but ſo little were the native miniſters themſelves, acquainted with this intricate buſineſs, that it was ſome years before they either thought of, or propoſed a remedy for the defects of their plan. It cannot, therefore, in any fairneſs of argument, be called the *Engliſh adminiſtration*. In 1769, the plan of *Engliſh ſupervisors* was adopted; and this was the firſt interference of *Engliſh adminiſtration* in the interior provinces. The Company's own lands, called the ceded lands, had been managed according to their own plan; and in the province of Burdwan, they had tried the ſyſtem of farming for a term of years: this was found to anſwer ſo well, that this country was as fine a garden, as your fa-

mous

mous one of Fyzoola Khan, or the "exquiſite "ſpot" of Tanjour. Obſerve, Sir, that one of theſe "obſcure young men" you ſo ſeverely cenſure, had the ſuperintendance of this diſtrict, and that its ſuperior cultivation and fertility, pointed it out as an example for the reſt of the country to be governed by; and the Directors repeatedly and earneſtly recommended the ſyſtem of letting out the lands of Bengal on leaſe, on account of the good effects produced by it in Burdwan. It was in conſequence of theſe orders of the Company, that Mr. Haſtings, when he became Governor of Bengal, propoſed the plan of letting the lands for a term of five years. This plan was maturely debated in council, by gentlemen who had been many years in the Company's ſervice. Particular regulations were framed, for the landholders and collectors: A regular plan for the adminiſtration of juſtice was alſo formed, whereby the method of obtaining it was greatly facilitated to the lower orders of people: The proceedings of the courts of juſtice, were ordered to be recorded, and conducted with a regularity unknown before: The courts of revenue, were alſo put on a better footing: The interior police of the country was regulated at the ſame time, on the ſame methodical grounds: And all theſe regulations were founded on the principles of the laws and cuſtoms of the Hindoos and Muſſulmen,

You ſay, Sir, in the ſame page, " No prefe-
" rence was given to the ancient proprietors; they
" muſt bid againſt every uſurer, every temporary
" adventurer, every jobber and ſchemer, every
" ſervant of every European, or they were obliged
" to content themſelves, in lieu of their extenſive
" domain, with their houſe, *and ſuch a portion as*
" *the ſtate auctioneers thought fit to aſſign.* In this
" general calamity, ſeveral of the firſt nobility
" thought (and in all appearance juſtly) that they
" had better ſubmit to the neceſſity of this penſion,
" than continue under the names of Zemindars,
" the objects and inſtruments of a ſyſtem, by
" which they ruined their tenants, and were ruin-
" ed themſelves." You never are ſo unfortunate, Sir, as when you come to *facts*; they puzzle you extremely; they are fit only for men of plain ſenſe and common honeſty, and are far beneath the attention of men of your ſublime genius. A perſon of plain underſtanding would ſuppoſe, that when you aſſert the nobility and gentry were ſet up to the higheſt bidder, they were expoſed to ſale along with their lands, like the villains of the feudal ſyſtem. Nothing can be ſo far from the truth. The reſt of your aſſertions, that no preference was given to ancient proprietors, and that they had only ſuch a penſion as the ſtate auctioneers thought fit to allow them, is equally void of foundation. Where the ancient proprietors offered an adequate rent for their lands, *they had the preference.* It was

the caſe in the largeſt zemindary in Bengal, namely, Rajeſhay.* It was the caſe in the inferior zemindaries and talookdories belonging to Moorſhadabad.† It was the caſe in the talooks of Kiſshennagur. It was the caſe in the numerous petty zemindaries and talookdories of Houghley. It was the caſe in the *whole of the provinces of Midnapore and Jellaſore.* And the Governor and Council have theſe remarkable words in their general letter to the Court of Directors, dated the 3d of November 1772; "The Huzzoor Zulahs, and the "inferior Zemindaries, bordering on Moorſhada-"bad and Rajeſhay, were alſo ſettled on the ſame "plan, [meaning Rajeſhay,] *a preference being al-*"*ways given to the offers of the hereditary poſſeſſors,* "*as before obſerved.*" With theſe authorities, allow me to uſe your own words; "Shall I be be-"lieved in relating it! You have, (Mr. Burke has,) endeavoured to miſlead the judgement of the Houſe of Commons and the nation, by a glaring falſe aſſertion In thoſe diſtricts where the Zemindars lands were let out to farm, the condition of the firſt nobility, as you are pleaſed to call them, was quite the reverſe of what your fancy has painted it. This plan of farming took from them no other hereditary right, than merely transferring the management of the collections to another hand; a thing that was frequently done in the Mogul go-

*General Letter, dated the 3d of November, 1772. †Ibid.

vernment

ment under another name, and almoſt univerſally by Coſſim Ally Khan. Their tenants were no otherwiſe affected, than that in many inſtances, they were better treated than by their own Zemindars. If you underſtood the ſyſtem at all, you would know, that whether a Zemindar or farmer hold the lands from government, the *inferior collectors are never changed.* Inſtead of having only their " houſe, and ſuch a penſion as the ſtate auctio-" neers allowed them," as you aſſert, they had the profits of all their alienated lands, under various denominations. They had their hereditary offices of check and controul, on the collections of the farmers. They had their allowance for ſervants of ſtate: And they had an allowance for their own maintenance, of ten per centum on the revenue, *agreeably to an ancient eſtabliſhed cuſtom of the country.* In ſhort, Sir, though the lands were leaſed for five years, inſtead of an annual ſettlement being made, and though, in a few zemindaries were their management was ſuperſeded for that term, yet the internal ſyſtem of collection, was not in the leaſt deviated from, and the whole plan was regulated according to the laws and cuſtoms of the country.

Warmed by the colouring of your own pencil, you proceed with more than ordinary heat, to ſay, " Such an univerſal proſcription, upon any pre-" tence, has few examples. Such a proſcription, " without

" without even a pretence of delinquency, has " none. It ſtands as a monument to aſtoniſh the " imagination, to confound the reaſon of man- " kind." I am ſure, Sir, I may ſay ſuch terms, on ſuch an occaſion, have no example. They are uſed merely to confound the reaſon and miſlead the judgement. If I underſtand the term *proſcription* rightly, it implies the idea either of death or confiſcation. Is there any thing like ſuch ſeverity in the ſimple act of leaſing lands for five years, without infringing any heriditary right of the Zemindars, and allowing them in common with others, to make their own propoſals, and granting them an ample ſtipend, if they did not chooſe to accept the terms of government? Such a manifeſt perverſion of terms, ſuch a wilful diſtortion of facts, is, indeed, " a monument " of the baſeſt deſign.

" I WAS in a manner ſtupified, by the deſperate " boldneſs of a few *obſcure young men*, who, hav- " ing obtained, by ways which they could not " comprehend, a power, of which they ſaw neither " the purpoſes nor the limits, toſſed about, ſub- " verted, and tore to pieces, as if it were in the " gambols of a boyiſh unluckineſs and malice, " the *moſt eſtabliſhed* rights, and the *moſt ancient* " and *moſt revered* inſtitution of ages." This paſſage is enough to ſtupify the ſenſes of any man, who does not know the " *deſperate boldneſs*" of an impudent faction. These *few obscure young men*, were a Governor and Council of nine Members, with the present Governor General for their President, who had been regularly bred to the Company's business, and had served them from fifteen to twenty years, consequently they could not have been very obscure, nor very young. The majority of them were well versed in the language, the laws, and customs of the country, and most of them had been employed in the very department they were about to regulate. The plan recommended to the attention of these gentlemen by the Court of Directors, was to assume openly, the management of the dewannee in the Company's name, without any foreign intervention. The ability with which they discharged this trust, does honour to their talents and industry. In the execution of these orders, the principal point of their duty, was the regulation of the revenues; and to perform this properly, their first care was to render the accounts of the revenue, simple and intelligible, to establish fixed rules for the collections, to make the mode of them uniform in all parts of the provinces, and to provide for an equal administration of justice. Their regulations for the first of these purposes, defined and explained the rights of the tenant and collector, ascertained the claims of the latter precisely and distinctly, and put an end to many oppressive exactions. Their admirable plan for the administration of justice, both civil and criminal, afforded

afforded the inhabitants a readier accefs to it, and gave form and permanency to a fyftem, which had hitherto been confufed and fluctuating. They abolifhed all vexatious taxes, of which there were many, both in revenue and trade. They inftituted a new mode of collecting the cuftoms, to the great relief of every merchant and inhabitant of the kingdom. In fhort, though this was one of the firft works of reformation in a new government, and a novel department, yet the plan was fo maturely confidered, fo judicioufly arranged, and fo wifely framed, that it obtained the admiration and applaufe of the Minifters and Directors; and was not only the bafis on which a future adminiftration founded their conduct, but a guide to the government of General Clavering, Colonel Monfon, and your great Lycurgus, Mr. Francis.

THE four fucceeding pages, are filled with much illiberal abufe: many injurious afperfions are caft on fome particular gentlemen, and hints of fraud and concealment, are thrown out againft the whole of the Company's government. The perfonal invective may perhaps be anfwered more particularly by fome of the parties at a future time; for the prefent I will, in juftice to the characters of fome of thefe much injured abfent gentlemen, defend them from the foul infinuations you have urged againft them. Your words are, "The "whole fubordinate Britifh adminiftration of re-

 venue,

" venue, was then veſted in a committee in Cal-
" cutta, *all creatures* of the Governor General."
This committee, Sir, whom you have ſo wantonly inſulted, conſiſted of the following members: *Mr. David Anderſon, Mr. John Shore, Mr. Charles Crofts, Mr. Samuel Charters, Mr. John Evelyn.* Theſe gentlemen have ſerved the Company from thirteen to ſixteen years, with credit to themſelves, and fidelity to their maſters. Some of them are poſſeſſed of eminent talents. Mr. Anderſon's conduct as an Ambaſſador to the Mahratta ſtates, is an ample and conſpicuous proof of this; and I am ſure Mr. Francis will give teſtimony to the diſtinguiſhed abilities of Mr. Shore. Mr. Crofts has had repeated aſſurances of approbation from his ſuperiors, for his accurate diſcharge of the important office of accountant-general to the revenue department, for the ſpace of ten years. Mr. Charters and Mr. Evelyn, are both well acquainted with the language of the country, and the nature of the revenues. They are all the ſons of gentlemen, and all their characters are the characters of gentlemen. They have always preſerved an unſullied reputation; and their nice ſenſe of honour and independence, would make them ſpurn at the degrading idea of being the *creature* of any man, however high his ſtation, with as much indignity, as they will deſpiſe the author of ſo baſe a calumny.

You

You conclude theſe indecent reproaches of the government in the following malignant terms: "In effect, Sir, every legal regular authority in "matters of revenue, of political adminiſtration, "of criminal law, of civil law, in many of the "moſt eſſential parts of military diſcipline, and in "oppreſſive, irregular, capricious, unſteady, ra-"pacious, and peculating deſpotiſm, with a direct "diſavowal of obedience to any authority at home, "and without any fixed maxim, principle, or rule "of proceeding, to guide them in India, is at "preſent the ſtate of your charter government "over great kingdoms." As you have dwelt much on "plans of concealment," "obſcure and "ſilent gulphs," "thickeſt ſhades of night," "clandeſtine government," and made frequent uſe of theſe dark and gloomy phraſes, to the great terror (as you hope) of many an honeſt man's imagination, I will endeavour to diſpel the fears you have created, by a ſimple narrative of this internal government, of which you have drawn ſo hideous a picture; and I am not without hopes, that a "plain tale may put you down."

In the year 1765, Lord Clive obtained the grant of the dewannee, which is the office of the miniſter who ſuperintends the lands and collections. Several circumſtances concurred to make his Lordſhip over rate the importance of the acquiſition, and the value of the gift. He conceived it

to

to be an inexhaustible mine of wealth, and not knowing the extent of its riches, he thought them unbounded. I will do his Lordship the justice to say, that I believe he meant not to deceive the Company, but was deceived himself. Hence it happened, that in a few years, when the springs of this vast source began to fail, the Company and the nation readily adopted the idea of mismanagement, and by a very easy association, concluded it was the fault of English government. Prejudice and envy carried the notion still further, and the terms of rapacity and oppression, were indiscriminately used, without caring about, or enquiring, into the justness of the application. It was deemed impossible, that the riches of such a kingdom as Bengal, should fail so soon; and as peculation and corruption were boldly asserted to be the causes, few or none gave themselves the trouble to ask for any other. These prejudices have been rather strengthened than abated since that period, and, I fear, like the force of habit, have increased by indulgence. Certain it is, however, that the seeds of those evils, which began to shew themselves soon after the acquisition of the dewannee, had been sown long before the English interference; and unfortunately for them, some general consequences, that must have happened in the common course of things, were thought to be the particular effects of their misconduct.

I HAVE already proved, from the teſtimony of two *hiſtorians, that when we came into poſſeſſion of theſe provinces, they had been ravaged by foreign invaſions and civil wars; that ancient eſtabliſhments had been overthrown, and the country groaned under every ſpecies of domeſtic confuſion. This confuſion predominated more in the department of the revenues, than any other: And from the invaſion of Nadir Shah, to the time I am ſpeaking of, "§new taxes, under new names, "were invented, which the landholder was oblig-"ed to levy on the tenants." The laſt Nabob, Coſſim Ally Khan, had the character of an able financier, and a ſevere collector; but he was a cunning, rather than a wiſe ſtateſman; and he procured an increaſe of revenue, more from the fear of his ſtrictneſs, than the wiſdom of his plans. One of his meaſures was the appointment of *aumils*, who were his own immediate officers of collection. Some of them had a joint power with the Zemindars, and ſome had a power totally independent of them; but in all caſes, they had a pernicious influence. The native miniſters, or rather Mahommed Reza Cawn, who had the ſuperintendance of the collections, ſeem not to have been aware of the evils of this ſyſtem for a conſiderable time. This may in ſome meaſure be accounted for; becauſe the buſineſs of the revenue was in-

*Scrafton and Dow. §Scrafton.

tricate,

tricate, and Mahommed Reza Cawn himſelf, was not ſo intimately acquainted with the detail of it, as to know its particular defects. In the year 1769, theſe aumils, who were moſt of them adventurers from Perſia, were pretty ‡ loudly complained of, as the authors of great oppreſſion, and the failure of the revenues became a matter of ſerious conſideration. Mr. Verelſt, who was then the Governor, having, in his own ſuperintendance of a province, proved the good effects of ſuch a controul, and having ſeen it in other inſtances in the Company's own lands, firſt adopted the idea of ſending Company's ſervants into the interior parts of the country, under the title of ſupervifors: And this is properly the era of *Engliſh adminiſtration*. In juſtice to the ſervice, and a ſet of gentlemen in that ſervice, who have been much injured by very ſevere and unjuſt reproaches, I wiſh it to be remarked, that the decay of the provinces had proceeded from extraneous cauſes, and that the evils complained of, aroſe from a number of circumſtances, with which they had no connection, and for which they could not be at all reſponſible;

The conſequences of thoſe wars and invaſions, before ſpoken of, were, that many rich ſtreams, through which wealth flowed into Bengal, had been

‡Select Committee's Letter, Auguſt the 16th, 1769

dried up. Raw ſilk, cloths, and other manufactures, to a vaſt amount, were diſperſed as far as Guzurat, Lahore, and even Iſpahan, before the irruption of Nadir Shah: And Mr. Verelſt has ſtated, from the cuſtom house books of Moorſhadabad, that nearly 70 lacks of rupees were brought into the provinces, for the purchaſe of raw ſilk alone. To this importation of wealth, muſt be added full as much from all the European nations, and merchants at Buſſorah and other places; the greateſt part of which had been put a total ſtop to before our government exiſted. But this was not the leaſt evil; for this great influx of wealth, which had been poured into the kingdom, and was the ſtock on which it maintained itſelf, was drained off by larger channels than it had flowed in. *It has been computed, that Coſſim Ally Khan robbed the country of near five millions ſterling, in jewells and ſpecie. China, Madraſs, and Bombay, were ſupplied from Bengal, to an enormous extent. The King's tribute, and the expence of a brigade at Allahabad, were alſo great ſums loſt to circulation. So that from theſe, and other concurrent cauſes, a rapid diminution of the riches of the country, is not to be wondered at.

THE internal management of the country, had been very defective for many years, as I have al-

*Mr. Verelſt's Letter, dated at Calcutta, April the 5th, 1769. Appendix of the Select Committee, 1773.

ready

ready ſhewn; and it was in this diſtracted and untoward ſituation of affairs, that the ſupervifors were ſent into the provinces, to endeavour to find out the cauſes of thoſe evils which exiſted in the collections, and to point out the means of correction. The gentlemen who were appointed to theſe important ſtations, did honour to their nomination. Much uſeful information was obtained from their reſearches, and many abuſes were detected by their vigilance. They opened the way to future improvements, and laid the foundation of a more regular ſyſtem. This was all which could be expected of them in the ſhort time of their adminiſtration; for notwithſtanding their great diligence, they had ſo many artifices to detect, and ſo many intricacies to unravel, that they were unable to do more than point out the abuſes they diſcovered, leaving the correction of them to more mature plans, which time alone could effect. The great objects of their appointment, and the moſt deſirable end to be obtained by it, were to find out, if poſſible, the methods by which the poor tenant was oppreſſed, in the firſt inſtance, by the collectors, and the embezzlements of them and the Zemindars. Government conceived, that it was defrauded of its juſt dues on the one hand, whilſt the tenants were oppreſſed on the other, by unauthorized exactions; and on this hinge turns the great art of collection; for if the rates which the Zemindar ſhould pay to government, could be well

well fixed, and the exact rent, with the articles on which it was raised, precisely ascertained, the motive for concealment of the real value of the lands by the Zemindar, and the means of oppression in the collector, would be removed. We shall see how nearly the plans in Mr. Hastings's government, have accomplished these purposes.

In the year 1772, when Mr. Hastings came to the government, the settlement which you have so unjustly arraigned, took place. *A preliminary step to its formation, was a thorough investigation of diverse complex articles, which had been introduced into the collections by the Nabobs, in order that such might be deducted from the rent roll, as *appeared most oppressive to the inhabitants.* †Another wise measure of the Council was, to endeavour to ascertain the claims on the inhabitants precisely, and also the value of the land. Hence it appears, that at the very outset of the business, they struck at the root of *concealment* and *oppression*, and began the work of reformation by the best possible method. I cannot elucidate the subject better, nor do them more justice, than by quoting their own words to the Court of Directors on the occasion.

*General Letter, dated the 3d of November, 1772. †Ibid.

" *Though ſeven years had elapſed ſince the " Company became poſſeſſed of the dewannee, " yet no regular proceſs had ever been formed for " conducting the buſineſs of the revenue. Every " zemindary, and every talook, was left to its " own particular cuſtoms. Theſe, indeed, were " not inviolably adhered to. The novelty of the " buſineſs to thoſe who were appointed to ſuperin- " tend it, the chicanery of the people whom they " were obliged to employ as their agents, the ac- " cidental exigencies of each diſtrict, and not un- " frequently the juſt diſcernment of the collector, " occaſioned many changes. Every change add- " ed to the confuſion which involved the whole, " and few were either authorized or known, by " the preſiding members of the government. The " articles which compoſed the revenue, the form " of keeping accounts, the computation of time, " even the technical terms, which ever form the " greateſt part of the obſcurity of every ſcience, " differed as much as the ſoil and productions of " the province. This confuſion had its origin in " the nature of the former government. The " Nazims exacted what they could from the Ze- " mindars and great farmers of the revenue, whom " they left at liberty to plunder all below, reſerv- " ing to themſelves the prerogative of plundering " them in their turn, when they were ſuppoſed to

*General Letter, dated the 3d of November, 1772.

" have enriched themſelves with the ſpoils of the " country. The Mutſuddies, who ſtood between " the Nazim and the Zemindars, or between them " and the people, had each their reſpective ſhares " of the public wealth. Theſe profits were conſi- " dered as illegal embezzlements, and therefore " were taken with every caution which could inſure " ſecrecy; and being conſequently fixed by no " rule, depended on the temper, abilities, or " power, of each individual, for the amount. It " therefore became a duty to every man, to take " the moſt effectual meaſures to conceal the value " of his property, and evade every enquiry into " his conduct, while the Zemindars and other " landholders, who had the advantage of long poſ- " ſeſſions, availed themſelves of it, by complex " diviſions of the lands, and intricate modes of " collection, to perplex the officers of government, " and confine the knowledge of the rents to them- " ſelves. It will be eaſily imagined, that much " of the current wealth ſtopped in its way to the " public treaſury.

" The internal management of each diſtrict, " varied no leſs than that of the whole province. " The lands ſubject to the ſame collection, and in- " termixed with each other, were ſome held by " farm, ſome ſuperintended by ſhicdars, or agents, " on the part of the collector, and ſome left to the " Zemindars or Talookdars themſelves, under

" various

" various degrees of controul. The firſt were " racked without mercy, becauſe the leaſes were " but of a year's ſtanding, and the farmer had no " intereſt or check, to reſtrain him from exacting " more than the land could bear: the ſecond were " equally drained, and the rents embezzled, as it " was not poſſible for the collector, with the " greateſt degree of attention on his part, to de- " tect or prevent it. The latter, it may be ſup- " poſed, were not exempted from the general cor- " ruption; if they were, the other lands which " lay near them, would ſuffer by the emigration " of their inhabitants, who would naturally ſeek " refuge from oppreſſion, in a milder and more " equitable government.

" SUCH was the ſtate of your revenue, when " your commands were received by the Lapwing, " and happily removed the difficulties which op- " poſed the introduction of a more perfect ſyſtem, " by aboliſhing the office of Naib Dewan, and au- " thorizing your adminiſtration to aſſume openly " the management of the dewannee in your name, " without any foreign intervention.

" IN the execution of theſe your intentions, the " points which claimed our principal attention, " as will appear by the above deſcription, were " *to render the accounts of the revenue ſimple and in-* " *telligible, to eſtabliſh fixed rules for the collections,*

" *to*

"*to make the mode of them uniform in all parts of*
"*the province, and to provide for the equal administra-*
"*tion of justice.*"

In order to secure the inhabitants in the quiet possession of their lands, and to prevent the exactions heretofore levied upon them, the Governor and Council then formed regulations for the observance of the Zemindars, farmers, and tenants, and established certain rules for the administration of justice. These regulations were replete with good sense, and displayed such an intimate knowledge on the subject of the revenues, that they have ever since been constantly referred to, for information and instruction. Soon after they had concluded the settlement of the lands, they adopted a new mode of managing them. They divided the provinces into six grand divisions: Each division was composed of a certain number of districts, and the charge of it committed to the care of a Chief and Council. Their duty was to receive the collections from the Zemindars or head farmers, to enquire into all complaints that might be made of a deviation from the rules laid down by the Governor and Council, to adjust any disputed claims or accounts between the Zemindar and his collectors, or between the collectors and the tenants, if the Zemindar himself did not redress them, and to administer justice in all cases of revenue and property.

This establishment lasted about eight years; that of supervisors or collectors, had continued three; so that in the course of this time, there was scarcely a species of abuse in the collections, which had not been referred to them, and of course afforded an instance of almost every evil and its remedy.

The Zemindars of every district had representatives in Calcutta. The Provincial Councils were obliged to send their proceedings to the Supreme Council every month, and every man in every village knew, that he might go either to the one or the other, for a redress of any grievance he had to complain of. The number of cases constantly referred to the Provincial Councils, and the appeals made to the Supreme Council at Calcutta, have so completely exposed and laid open all this mystery of collection, the value of the lands has also been so nearly ascertained from a variety of local investigations, and all the intricacies of fraud and embezzlement in the native collectors, have been so accurately traced out, that a person in London (to use your own phrase) may, by reading the Company's records, be a competent judge of what has been done in the provinces of Bengal, Bahar, and Orissa.

The great purposes of ascertaining the value of the lands, and detecting the various abuses of the collections,

collections, being thus nearly accomplished, all oppressive taxes being abolished, and the revenues actually defined and clearly explained, Mr. Hastings and his Council chose that fit opportunity of recalling the Provincial Councils, and fixing the seat of collections at Calcutta. This particular department they as wisely committed to the management of a separate Board, who have handsome salaries allowed them, and are sworn not to take any other emoluments than the avowed allowance of office. The Zemindars, or head farmers, now make all their settlements with this Board (subject to the controul and approbation of the Supreme Council) at the Presidency, amidst a numerous body of people, both Europeans and natives, all acquainted *now* with the nature of the revenues, and many of them with the value of the very lands so let. Is this a plan of concealment? All their accounts of every kind, are regularly kept: They are liable to check and controul in various offices. Is this like an obscure and silent gulph? Every Member of Council may, if he pleases, inform himself of the various articles of revenue; and there is not a man in the kingdom, who may not, if he is desirous of it, lay his complaints before him. Is this no means of detecting fraud and or mismanagement? The Zemindars now make their own agreements in their own lands, and are no longer subject to the interference of either European or Persian collectors. Neither are they

E any

any longer afraid of increaſing demands from government, or of any arbitrary impoſitions on the revenue: It is, therefore, their intereſt to encourage cultivation, and protect their inhabitants. If any of their tenants are aggrieved by the farmers to whom the lands are let, they apply to them for redreſs, and they can appeal to Calcutta, if they are not ſatisfied. The plan of the criminal courts, is an ancient eſtabliſhment, or in your emphatical term, a *revered inſtitution*, revived; and the civil courts of juſtice, are regulated on a more extenſive ſcale than they were before, which renders the acceſs to them ſtill more eaſy.

THIS is a very ſummary and imperfect ſketch of the many admirable regulations and improvements in the management of the revenues, which are to be found in the Company's records; and whoever wiſhes to meet with ample information on this ſubject, will there find it; and will alſo find, that there is not one word of truth in all you have aſſerted, of ſilent gulphs, thickeſt ſhades, and plans of concealment. If any Member of Parliament, ſhould by chance meet with, and read this performance, I hope it will be an hint to him, not to truſt to bold aſſertions in the Houſe, nor believe them the more for their being made by a member of any particular committee. I hope alſo, it may ſuggeſt to him an idea of the neceſſity of that doctrine, which was ſo frequently preſſed

preſſed on the Houſe, namely, prove the abuſe before you conſent to puniſh it.

And now, Sir, having remarked on as much of your ſpeech, as I have time or patience to attend to, permit me to exerciſe a little of that ſort of freedom, in which you have indulged yourſelf rather licentiouſly, both on bodies of men, and individual characters. Allow me to enquire, if your public conduct has been ſo guided by that ſtrict rule of morality, and ſo ſquared by that exact mode of faith which you profeſs, as never to have infringed " the *covenant*, *the ſolemn, original,* " *indiſpenſable oath, in which you are bound by the* " *eternal frame and conſtitution of things, to the whole* " *human race?*"* Let me then aſk you, Sir, if you do not take a *ſolemn oath*, that you are *bona fide* poſſeſſed of three hundred pounds a year, when you take your ſeat in Parliament, and whether you always have poſſeſſed that qualification, ever ſince you had your ſeat in Parliament? Let me aſk you, if you did not protect and reſtore to office, a public defaulter, giving as a reaſon to the Houſe for ſo doing, that it was on account of his great knowledge of, and capacity for buſineſs, in that office? and whether in a little time, you did not take a *ſolemn oath*, that you believed him to be inſane, and incapable of any buſineſs, from a

*Vide Mr. Burke's Speech, page 67.

period

period that was previous to your aforesaid public declaration? Have you ever gambled in the stocks; and has your conduct therein, ever been the subject of legal prosecution? Have you, in any instance of your life, indulged a malevolent propensity (you seem to have) and depreciated the character of an absent person? And upon a friend of that person being informed of the liberty you had taken, and expostulating with you, did you not come to a satisfactory explanation? Perhaps a little self examination of this kind, may induce you to "bear your faculties more meekly," and learn you to think, that the Company's servants are not the only persons in the world, who want reformation.

I am, Sir, &c. &c.

[illegible] END.

www.ingramcontent.com/pod-product-compliance
Lightning Source LLC
Chambersburg PA
CBHW021433090426
42739CB00009B/1469
9783337059217